KT-431-948

It's Your Health!

Alcohol

JILLIAN POWELL

W
FRANKLIN WATTS
LONDON·SYDNEY

First published in 2004 by Franklin Watts
96 Leonard Street, London EC2A 4XD

Franklin Watts Australia
45-51 Huntley Street
Alexandria, NSW 2015

Series editor: Sarah Peutrill
Designed by: Pewter Design Associates
Series design: Peter Scoulding
Illustration: Mike Atkinson and Guy Smith, Mainline Design
Picture researcher: Diana Morris
Series consultant: Wendy Anthony, Health Education Unit, Education Service, Birmingham City Council
Picture credits:
Paul Almasy/Corbis: 39b. Paul Baldesare/Photofusion: Posed by models: front cover. John Birdsall Photography: 32c. British Museum, London/Werner Forman Archive: 10t. BSIP, Gounot/SPL: 17t. BSIP, Laurent H. Americain/SPL: 24c. Oscar Burriel/SPL: 29b. CC Studio/SPL: 23b. Chat Magazine/Rex Features: 40c. Robert Essel NYC/Corbis: 27b. Chris Fairclough: 4, 19, 21t, 26, 41, 45. Jon Feingersh/Corbis: 8t. Peter M. Fisher/Corbis: 34b. Owen Franken/Corbis: 8b. John van Hassel/Corbis: 37t. Gary Houlder/Corbis: 12t. Jutta Klee/Corbis: 15b. Bob Krist/Corbis: 25t. Chris Lisle/Corbis: 12b. Tom & Dee Ann McCarthy/Corbis: 33b. Minnesota Historical Society/Corbis: 10b. Amet Jean Pierre/Corbis: 37b John Powell/Rex Features: 18t. Charles O'Rear/Corbis: 36c. Chuck Savage/Corbis: 25b. Isopress Senepart (SEN)/Rex Features: 31b. Shepard Sherbell/Corbis SABA: 30c. S.I.N/Corbis: 28c. Peter Turnley/Corbis: 13b. Underwood & Underwood/Corbis: 11t. Garry Watson/SPL: 22c. Michael S. Yamashita/Corbis: 35c.

The Publisher would like to thank the Brunswick Club for Young People, Fulham, London for their help with this book. Thanks to our models, including Spencer Thoroughgood, Stevie Waite and Eva Webb.

A CIP catalogue record for this book is available from the British Library.

ISBN 0 7496 5570 4

Printed in Malaysia

Contents

What is alcohol?

Alcohol is the most widely used drug in the world. Like nicotine in tobacco and caffeine in coffee, alcohol can affect our body and mind, changing the way we feel. It is also an addictive drug – we can come to depend on it and need it. But unlike addictive drugs such as heroin and cocaine, alcohol is a legal and socially-accepted drug, used all over the world.

Alcohol is a normal part of social life for many of us. ▲

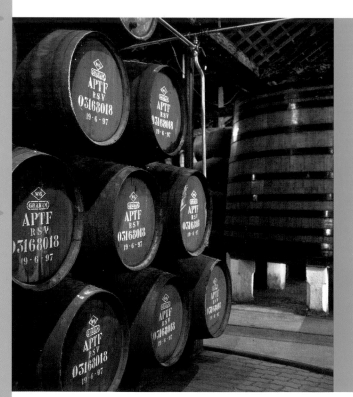

▲ Wines, port and spirits may all be stored in oak vats to mature.

How is alcohol made?

Alcohol is made from fruit, vegetables or grains by a process called fermentation. During fermentation, yeasts (tiny microbes) in fruit or grain grow as they feed on sugars and starches, producing ethanol (alcohol) and the gas carbon dioxide. Yeasts stop growing when the alcoholic strength reaches 14 per cent, but purer alcohol can be made by a process called distillation.

In distillation, the fermented liquid is heated and, as alcohol boils at a lower temperature than water, it escapes as a vapour. The vapour is cooled so that it distills and turns back into liquid alcohol. This process is used to make alcoholic spirits such as whisky and brandy. Some spirits are then stored or matured for ten years or more, improving their flavour.

Alcoholic drinks

Alcoholic drinks come in a wide range of flavours, colours and smells. Some flavours come from the fruit or grain. Cider gets its flavour from apples, beer from barley or hops, wine usually from grapes, and whisky from malted grain. Substances called congeners may also be added to give flavour, colour and smell.

Alcoholic content

The strength of alcoholic drinks is measured as the percentage of alcohol by volume (abv): the higher the percentage, the stronger the drink. The alcoholic strength depends on the amount of yeast used, the time allowed for fermentation, distillation and storage. Percentage of alcohol by volume ranges from 0.03 per cent (non-alcoholic lagers) to 44.8 per cent abv (some Polish and Russian vodkas). The law requires the alcoholic content to be shown on labels.

Lagers range in strength from non- or low-alcohol to 9 per cent for special brews.

Drinks labels show the percentage of alcohol content by volume (abv).

It's your experience

'Everyone drinks, don't they? Even your aunt. They all have their own tipple. It's just part of social life, really.'

Sam, aged 18

It's your opinion

Some people think that it is unfair that some addictive drugs get a bad press while alcohol is socially acceptable, although it can be just as harmful to health. Should alcohol be classed with drugs like tobacco and cannabis, and given the same health warnings?

Alcohol in the past

Alcohol is one of the oldest and most widely used drugs in history. Its use dates back to around 8,000BCE. For thousands of years, alcohol was seen as safer to drink than water. It was used as medicine, as an antiseptic for wounds and as a tonic for the sick.

This engraving from around 2500BCE shows wine being drunk at a banquet in the Middle East.

Everyday life and ceremony

As early as 5,000BCE, grain crops were grown in Ancient China and Egypt to make alcohol. In Ancient China, alcohol (*jiu*) was seen as bringing happiness and wealth. Wine was widely drunk in Ancient Greece and Rome. In the Roman army, soldiers were expected to drink wine to keep them healthy and make them less likely to catch diseases.

Alcohol has also played an important part in religion. The Ancient Egyptians, Greeks and Romans all had gods of wine, and wine is still used in Jewish and Christian ceremonies.

Temperance

In some countries, as industry changed people's lives in the nineteenth century, alcohol came to be seen as a threat to society. It was blamed for crime, poverty and high death rates and there were attempts to reduce and even ban its consumption. In the UK, the Temperance Movement was started in 1832 by a weaver called Joseph Livesey, who spoke out against the evils of gin dens and beer houses. At its height, one in ten people in the UK had 'taken the pledge' to drink no alcohol, and become 'teetotal'.

American women campaigning for Prohibition in 1917.

Police inspecting illegal stores of alcohol during Prohibition.

Prohibition

In the USA, a total ban on the making, selling and drinking of alcohol was introduced in 1920. The government hoped to improve people's health. Prohibition lasted until 1933 and banned all alcohol except for medicinal or religious purposes. It led to a thriving black market run by 'bootleggers' who made alcohol illegally, stole it from government warehouses, and smuggled it from overseas.

Criminal gangs controlled the alcohol business, opening up illegal drinking houses called 'speakeasies'. People hid alcohol in hip flasks, false books, hollow canes and anything else they could find. Prohibition did not have the desired effect – people drank more than ever before.

It's your decision

Do you want to be teetotal?
Some people are encouraging young people to 'take the pledge' and say no to drugs altogether – including alcohol. They argue that drugs are harmful to health, and cause many problems in society.

It's your opinion

Prohibition was an attempt to protect people from the evils of drink – but it only drove the alcohol business underground. Do you think there is anything governments can do today to stop people drinking too much?

Social drinking

In many countries around the world, alcohol is seen as an important part of relaxation and social life. Drinking is a social activity, with pubs, clubs and bars acting as places to meet, relax and have fun. Alcohol is used for partying and celebrations, from important occasions like weddings, to enjoying the weekend break from work.

Drinking alcohol is common on Hen and Stag nights. Drinking challenges and competitions encourage heavy drinking.

Drinking places

Drinking places can have their own national character, from the *bar-brasserie* in France and the country pub in the UK, to the *mapalu* in Zaire – a small clearing in the forest, dedicated to the drinking of palm wine. All are places where people interact and bond socially. In some countries they can be an important part of the community. In Poland, the tavern, or *karczma*, is where contracts are signed, village disputes settled, and marriages arranged.

French bars and cafés often spill out onto the pavements.

It's your experience

'You can't have a party without getting the beers in. What sort of party would that be? You need a drink to get everyone relaxed — in the mood. A party without booze — that would be a disaster!'

Greg, aged 19

It's your opinion

'Happy Hours' with cut-price drinks encourage people to get together and socialise after work. But they can also encourage binge drinking as drinkers try to make the most of discount prices — so much so that happy hours may be banned in Scotland. Do you think promotions like this are a good idea or not? Should it be left to individuals to decide how much they want to drink?

Celebrations

All over the world, alcohol is drunk to celebrate major life events. In many countries, people have a drink 'to wet the baby's head'. In Peru, *chicha* (maize beer) is drunk to mark lifecycle events from baptisms and confirmations, to birthdays, marriages and funerals. In Europe, champagne toasts are drunk to celebrate marriages and graduations, job promotions and retirement parties.

Social bonding

Different types of drink can bond social groups, classes and even nations – such as Guinness in Ireland, tequila in Mexico, whisky in Scotland and ouzo in Greece. In Europe, Australia and the USA, wine is often drunk with meals, while beer is popular for informal get-togethers. Teenagers often drink the same brands of drink to mark their membership of a social group.

Marriages are toasted with alcohol the world over.

What happens when we drink?

When we drink alcohol, it takes about ten minutes for the alcohol to travel from the stomach and intestine into our bloodstream. From here, it travels to every part of the body and brain.

How quickly?

The age, sex and size of the drinker affect how quickly alcohol is absorbed into the bloodstream, and how quickly the drinker becomes drunk. Eating food before drinking will slow down the absorption; taking other drugs can speed it up.

Blood vessels

Alcohol causes blood vessels in our skin to dilate (become wider) so that blood passes through them faster and we feel warm and look flushed.

Brain

As the alcohol reaches our brain, it slows down the links between our brain cells and other cells. At first, we start to feel more relaxed and confident. As we go on drinking, our body and brain work less efficiently. We may start to slur our words, lose concentration, and even fall over.

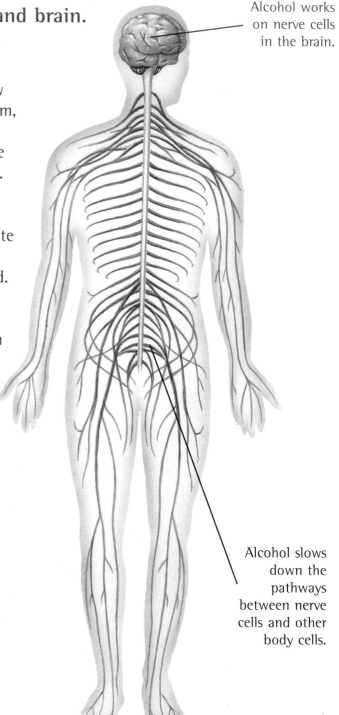

Alcohol works on nerve cells in the brain.

Alcohol slows down the pathways between nerve cells and other body cells.

It's your experience

'When my parents have a party they always drink too much. The way they act is really embarrassing – why can't they enjoy themselves without alcohol?'

Georgina, aged 13

Kidneys

When we drink the kidneys make us pass more urine, to flush out toxins from the alcohol. This can make us feel thirsty and dehydrated which may make us drink more.

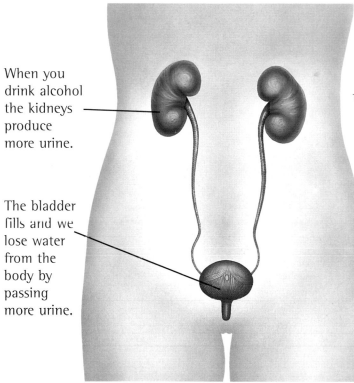

When you drink alcohol the kidneys produce more urine.

The bladder fills and we lose water from the body by passing more urine.

The kidneys filter about 1.2 litres of blood every minute. From it they extract unwanted substances – such as the toxins in alcohol – and excess water and salt to form urine, which goes to the bladder.

Why alcohol affects people differently

Women generally get drunk more quickly than men because they have smaller bodies that are less able to absorb alcohol. Women's bodies have less water and more fatty tissue than men's bodies. When a woman drinks the same amount as a man, the alcohol is less diluted by water, so her blood alcohol levels rise faster. Women may also have lower levels of an enzyme that breaks alcohol down.

Breaking alcohol down

Our body gets rid of ten per cent of alcohol in our breath and urine, but the rest has to be broken down by our liver so it can be removed from the body. The liver can only break down about one unit of alcohol in an hour (a small glass of wine or half a pint of beer). If we drink more than this, blood alcohol levels continue to rise as alcohol builds up in the bloodstream, and we get drunk.

It's your decision

Do you want to keep up with the men? As well as getting drunk faster, women feel the effects longer and are more likely to suffer liver damage from heavy drinking.

Some surveys suggest that a third of women now 'out-drink' men.

Sensible drinking

Experts agree that drinking alcohol in moderation does no harm to our body. In many countries government health advice sets recommended limits for sensible drinking. This is a level that poses a low risk of alcohol-related problems for the drinker and for others.

Safe drinking levels

UK (units – see below)	USA	Australia
Men:	**Men:**	**Men:**
21 units a week	2 alcoholic drinks a day	4 alcoholic drinks a day
Women:	**Women:**	**Women:**
14 units a week	1 alcoholic drink a day	2 alcoholic drinks a day
Teenagers:		
4 units a week		

A unit of alcohol is eight grammes of pure alcohol, which is:
- A single measure (25 ml) of spirits
- A small glass (50 ml) of sherry or fortified wine
- A small glass (125 ml) of wine
- Half a pint of beer, cider or lager

How much is enough?

The table above shows how much three national governments recommend men and women can safely drink.

It's your decision

Do you prefer to ignore health guidelines? In the UK, one in three men and one in five women drink more than the recommended limits each week, and are putting their health at risk.

Sensible drinking rules

Health experts also advise against binge drinking – drinking more than six units in a session for a woman, and eight for a man. This sort of drinking is very harmful as the liver is unable to break down large amounts of alcohol at a time.

If we do have too much to drink, the advice is to have no more alcohol for at least 48 hours to give the body time to recover. All governments recommend one or two alcohol-free days every week. These can help you keep control of your drinking and make it less likely to become a habit.

Most doctors recommend that pregnant women drink no alcohol at all.

When to say 'no'

Sometimes the only safe limit is no alcohol at all. Women who are pregnant (see page 23), and people who are driving or doing other jobs that need them to be alert and skilled, should drink no alcohol at all.

Alcohol should also be avoided by people with a personal or family history of harmful drinking, people with health problems such as diabetes, and people who are taking other drugs that could interact with alcohol.

It's your experience

'I make it a rule to alternate every alcoholic drink with a soft drink or a glass of water. It helps you keep a check on what you are drinking, and you get less dehydrated too.'

Maggie, aged 19

Being drunk

If we drink more alcohol than our body can cope with, we become drunk. This happens when blood alcohol levels reach around 100 milligrams of alcohol per 100 millilitres of blood. Being drunk changes our mood and behaviour. It affects our judgement, giving us a false sense of confidence and daring which can put our health and safety at risk.

Loss of control

As alcohol slows down our brain activity, we become clumsy and confused. When we are drunk, we are at greater risk of injuries such as falling over, or being involved as a pedestrian in a traffic accident.

Alcohol can also make us more emotional. We can become over-affectionate, sad, aggressive and violent. Drunks may get involved in fights, domestic violence and other criminal behaviour.

Alcohol and sex

When we are drunk, we are more likely to do things that put us at risk. Women who have been drinking heavily may lose their inhibitions and take risks like going home with a stranger, putting themselves in danger of being attacked or raped.

Drinking too much alcohol can lead to unsafe sex and unwanted pregnancies.

Drinking alcohol reduces our inhibitions – this can increase the risk of having unsafe sex.

It's your experience

'I was 14 when I first had sex. I'd had too much to drink, and I didn't know what I was doing. I really regret it now, because he meant nothing to me and I did want it to be special.'

Karly, aged 16

Many people admit to having unsafe sex after drinking too much alcohol. A US survey showed that 23 per cent of young people aged 15 to 24 admit to having unsafe sex after taking alcohol or drugs.

Blood alcohol levels

Our body responds to alcohol in stages. As blood alcohol levels rise, we may start to feel confused and dizzy. We become less co-ordinated, and our speech becomes slurred. If blood alcohol levels continue to rise, we will eventually be unable to stand or walk, we may start to vomit, and even lose consciousness.

▼ Extreme alcohol poisoning can lead to unconsciousness – without hospital treatment it can lead to death.

It's your decision

▶ Is a drink a good way to lose your inhibitions? Many young people say they are more likely to have unsafe sex after drinking. Unsafe sex can lead to unwanted pregnancies as well as to sexually transmitted diseases including HIV and AIDs. Think beyond the immediate effects of drinking to have a good time.

At blood alcohol levels of between 0.35 per cent and 0.50 per cent, the heart rate can slow and the body can fall into a coma. If they reach over 0.50 per cent, we may stop breathing and die. Some deaths are caused by alcohol poisoning, others by drunks choking on their own vomit.

Hangovers

When our body takes in too much alcohol, the result can be a 'hangover' the next day. The effects of a hangover can last 24 hours or more. They include feeling sick, thirsty, shaky and dizzy, and having a thumping headache.

Causes

Alcohol acts as a diuretic – which means it speeds up the rate at which our body loses water. The kidneys (see page 15) act to flush out toxins in alcohol by making us pass more urine. In the process they take water from our brain and body tissues, which may lead to a nasty headache.

Alcohol also contains toxins, which can act as mild poisons. Drinks like red wine, brandy and whisky are worse than colourless drinks like white wine and vodka, because they contain toxic substances called congeners.

Finally alcohol can also irritate the stomach lining, which can lead to vomiting.

Coloured drinks like red wine contain substances which can increase the risk of hangovers.

Avoiding hangovers

The best way to avoid hangovers is not to drink too much alcohol, especially large amounts in a short time. Eating a fatty meal or drinking a glass of milk before drinking can help as fat is digested slowly, so it lines and protects the stomach and slows down the absorption of alcohol.

Alternating alcoholic drinks with water or soft drinks helps reduce dehydration but fizzy drinks should be avoided as they increase the amount of alcohol that gets into the bloodstream. Mixing alcoholic drinks (such as beer or cider with spirits) will also make hangovers worse.

Another way to avoid a hangover is to drink lots of water and some orange juice before going to bed. The vitamin C in the juice helps speed up the rate at which the liver can break down alcohol.

Drinking milk helps slow down the rate at which our bodies absorb alcohol.

It's your experience

'Every time I wake up with a hangover, I think, "That's it, I'm never drinking again." But you do. You get wrecked, and you've no one to blame but yourself.'

Kelly, aged 17

Fruit juice containing vitamin C can help the liver break down alcohol. Eggs help to reduce toxins in the liver.

The liver breaks alcohol down at the rate of around one unit per hour.

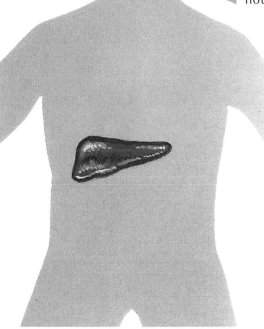

Hangover cures

Many people have their own hangover cures – ranging from tomato juice to pickled cucumbers or even having another drink. Water and vitamin C will help the body recover from dehydration and loss of important nutrients and vitamins. Eggs contain a chemical called cysteine, which is believed to mop up the toxins that build up in the liver while it is breaking alcohol down.

Some people take painkillers for headaches and to settle the stomach, but it is worth remembering that all drugs contain toxins, making the liver work even harder.

It's your decision

Will another drink help?
When the body is 'hung-over' it has overdosed on a depressant drug – alcohol. A 'hair of the dog' – having another drink – may steady the nerves for a while, but it's only adding to the body's overload of alcohol.

Health risks and benefits

The World Health Organisation lists alcohol as a leading health risk worldwide. Alcohol abuse causes around four per cent of disease globally, and 1.8 million deaths each year. Heavy drinking can affect nearly every part of the body, causing liver and brain damage, high blood pressure and strokes, and some cancers.

Liver disease can lead to jaundice, which turns body tissues yellow.

Liver damage

The liver has many vital functions in our body. It acts like a chemical factory, extracting what we need from our food and drink and filtering out toxins. It helps us break down alcohol, but long-term heavy drinking damages the liver so it is no longer able to function properly. Liver disease is called cirrhosis. Its symptoms include poor health, yellow skin and jaundice. It can eventually lead to coma and death.

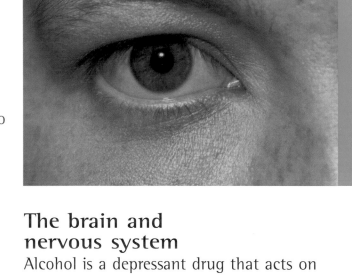

The brain and nervous system

Alcohol is a depressant drug that acts on the central nervous system that controls our heart rate and breathing. Heavy drinking can cause blackouts and confusion, and damage the part of the brain that co-ordinates movement. Long-term use can cause brain cells to shrink and die faster, and result in memory loss, dizziness and sight problems.

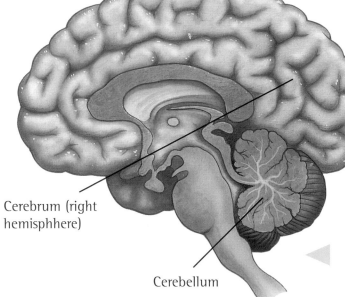

Cerebrum (right hemisphhere)

Cerebellum

The cerebellum is part of the brain that works with the cerebrum to regulate smooth body movements. It also helps to make sure that we stay balanced. If the cerebellum is damaged by alcohol we are not able to control the body properly.

Alcohol in pregnancy

When a woman is pregnant, alcohol from her bloodstream is absorbed by the developing baby. The baby is most sensitive to alcohol in the early stages of pregnancy when its nervous system and vital organs are being formed.

Research suggests that drinking alcohol can increase the risk of miscarriage or having an underweight baby. If the mother drinks over 56 units of alcohol a week, the baby may suffer problems with its growth and central nervous system and suffer from hyperactivity and learning difficulties. A study by Washington University found that young people whose mothers had got drunk at least once during their pregnancy, have a much higher chance of alcohol problems themselves.

▼ Blood pressure can be raised by stress, smoking and drinking alcohol.

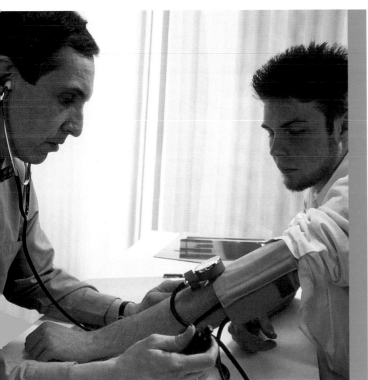

Cancer

Long-term heavy drinking has been linked to breast cancer in women, as well as cancers of the mouth, liver and lungs. The risk increases if the drinker is also a smoker.

Health benefits

Some studies suggest that drinking moderate amounts of alcohol may have some health benefits. Red wine, in particular, contains substances that help open up the coronary arteries, reducing the risk of strokes and heart attacks. For men over 40 and women after the menopause (who are at higher risk of heart disease) one unit of alcohol a day may lower the risk of heart attacks and heart disease. It may also help protect older women against osteoporosis. Heavy drinking, however, can cause high blood pressure and so increase the risk of coronary heart disease and strokes.

Alcoholism

Alcohol is an addictive drug, which means that if we drink too heavily too often, our bodies start to need alcohol in order to feel normal. This is called alcohol dependence, or alcoholism. Alcoholics feel that they cannot cope without alcohol. The amount they are drinking will start to cause problems in their health, work and relationships, but they are unable to stop drinking heavily because of their addiction.

Causes

Factors such as stress, the influence of friends, and the easy availability of alcohol, can all lead to alcoholism.

Some people are more likely to become addicted because their bodies lack certain chemicals and so cannot break alcohol down as efficiently as other people's.

Alcoholism can also sometimes run in families, and scientists are searching for a gene that could make people more likely to become alcoholics.

Scientists are studying the links between genes and addictive behaviour, including alcoholism.

It's your decision

Will drinking help your troubles? We all go through tough times in our lives – times when we feel sad or lonely or confused. Having a drink may help us forget our troubles for a while, but the problem will still be there, and this kind of drinking could lead to addiction.

Symptoms

An alcoholic is unable to control the amount they drink. They feel a constant craving or need to drink, and as their body becomes more tolerant of alcohol, they need to drink more and more to feel the same effects.

If they are suddenly unable to drink, they have withdrawal symptoms, which can include anxiety, shaking, sweating, sickness, convulsions and mood changes. These are signs that the brain and the liver are no longer able to cope with the smaller amount of alcohol in the body.

Support groups can help alcoholics to recover from their addiction.

Treatment

Alcoholics may need medical help to stop drinking. They may need to go into a clinic or hospital for a 'detoxification' programme, which rids the body of toxins from alcohol.

Tranquillisers are sometimes given to help their body overcome withdrawal symptoms in the first few days. Alcoholics may also be given drugs that reduce their craving for alcohol or which cause sickness immediately alcohol is drunk. Their stomach and liver may need treatment, and in severe cases a liver transplant may be needed.

Alcoholics may also need help to cope with problems such as stress, loneliness and unhappiness, which have led to their dependence on alcohol. This can be given by a professional counsellor and in support groups where other alcoholics and recovered alcoholics help each other.

It's your opinion

Alcohol – like tobacco – is an addictive drug that can harm health and even kill. Some people think alcohol labels should carry health warnings, like cigarette packets. Do you think this would help to stop people from becoming alcoholics?

For many alcoholics, drink is a way of trying to escape emotional problems.

Teenage drinking

Recent reports by the World Health Organisation and other research bodies show that teenagers are starting to drink earlier and more heavily than ever before. Drinking has become an important part of youth culture. Young people drink to bond with friends, to lift their mood and to cope with stress.

Alcopops and designer beers have encouraged young people to start drinking earlier.

Designer drinks and alcopops

The most popular drinks among teens include beer, lager, cider and spirits. Some designer brands are seen as a style statement. Alcohol companies also target young people with Alcopops, which are soft drinks such as cola or lemonade which have alcohol added.

It's your experience

'I don't really think about the future and health problems and stuff. You think it's never going to happen to you. You're just out to have a good time, that's all. It's usually Friday and Saturday nights that are the big nights, sometimes Sundays too.'

Gemma, aged 19

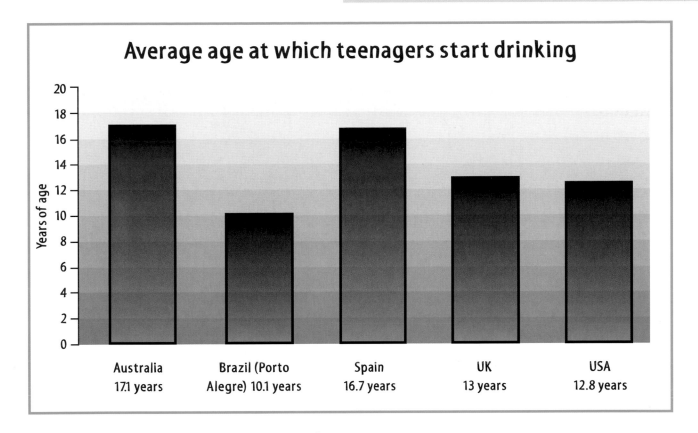

Average age at which teenagers start drinking

Years of age

| Australia | Brazil (Porto | Spain | UK | USA |
| 17.1 years | Alegre) 10.1 years | 16.7 years | 13 years | 12.8 years |

Long-term effects

Some studies show that regular heavy drinking may damage young people's brains and have long-term effects on learning and memory. As they get older, people who have started drinking early are likely to drink more heavily, and face more health and social problems. Young people who begin drinking before the age of 15 are four times more likely to develop alcohol dependence than those who begin drinking at the age of 21. There is also evidence that early heavy drinking is linked with crime and anti-social behaviour.

It's your decision

Is binge drinking worth it?

Regular binge drinking has been linked with strokes, kidney damage, memory loss and increased risk of breast cancer in women. Binge drinking is harmful because it builds up high concentrations of alcohol in the body, and alcohol is a poison.

Unsafe drinking among women aged 16 to 24 has more than doubled in the past decade. ▶

Alcohol and drugs

When we drink alcohol, we are taking a depressant drug that affects our central nervous system. If we take other drugs at the same time, the alcohol in our body can interact with them, sometimes in ways that are harmful to our health.

Club culture encourages some people to drink and take recreational drugs – which can be a fatal combination.

Alcohol can make some drugs stronger; it can also stop other drugs from working properly. Alcohol is known to interact with over 150 other kinds of drug, in ways that can cause illness, injury and even death.

Alcohol and recreational drugs

Alcohol is a 'recreational drug' that people take to lift their mood and help them enjoy themselves. Some people think that drinking alcohol can encourage people to try out other recreational drugs that are illegal, such as ecstasy and cocaine.

Mixing alcohol with these drugs can be very dangerous; alcohol is a factor in most deaths caused by ecstasy. This is because both drugs dehydrate the body and the combination can lead to overheating, coma and death. Mixing drugs can also cause long-term problems such as confusion and memory loss.

Alcohol and medicines

Alcohol increases the effects on the body of other depressant drugs including sleeping pills, tranquillisers, anti-depressants and some painkillers. This can cause drowsiness and an increased risk of damage to our body and brain.

Alcohol should be avoided when you need to take any other drugs such as painkillers.

It's your opinion

Alcohol is a legal and socially-accepted drug, unlike Class A drugs such as ecstasy, heroin and cocaine. But alcohol is an addictive drug, known to cause 40 per cent of all violent crime, and many more people become addicted to alcohol than to other drugs. Do you agree with the argument that alcohol is just as harmful as some illegal drugs?

The painkiller Tylenol can cause sudden liver failure if taken with alcohol. Paracetamol can also cause liver damage, and aspirin can cause stomach bleeding when combined with alcohol.

Drinking alcohol can cause sickness when someone is taking antibiotics to clear an infection. It can also reduce their effectiveness.

Alcohol can also be dangerous when combined with medication for conditions such as diabetes or heart disease.

It's your decision

Do you trust strangers?
Accepting a drink from a stranger carries the risk that it may be 'spiked' with other drugs. These can include Rohypnol, the 'date rape' drug that may be used to force a girl to have unwanted sex. Keeping an eye on everything you drink, or going out with a 'drink buddy' and keeping an eye out for each other, is one way of helping yourself stay safe.

The hidden costs of drinking

Alcohol abuse has heavy economic and social costs. Health services worldwide spend billions of pounds each year treating alcohol-related injuries and illnesses. Billions more are lost in poor productivity at work and in clearing up alcohol-related crime and social problems.

Alcohol abuse causes thousands of injuries and deaths each year.

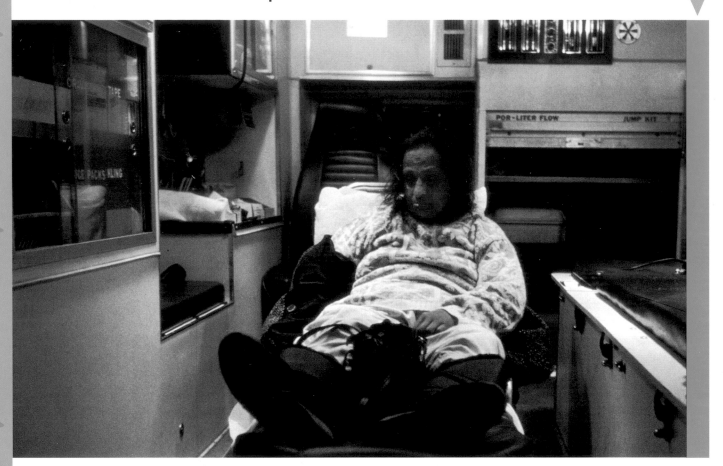

Health

Alcohol-related illnesses and emergencies cost billions of pounds each year. They include Accident and Emergency admissions such as glassings (cuts and injuries causes by broken bottles), road accidents, assaults and alcohol poisoning.

In the US, 23 per cent of drivers aged between 16 and 19 who were fatally injured in car crashes had high blood alcohol concentration (bac) of 0.10 per cent or more. Alcohol also causes premature deaths as a result of liver problems, heart disease and some cancers.

Employment

Alcohol costs billions in lost productivity due to hangovers and drink-related illnesses. In the US, around 500 million working days are lost each year because of alcohol problems – costing over $80 billion. In many countries employers report alcohol abuse among their employees, resulting in time off, poor performance, and accidents in the workplace.

Of course, alcohol also creates jobs – through its manufacture and sale. Governments also rely on it for the money it raises through taxation.

Social costs

Alcohol can be a major factor in family break-up. Marriages where one or both partners have a drink problem are twice as likely to end in divorce as those not affected. Children who live in families affected by drink problems are more likely to be neglected. Alcoholism can also lead to job loss and homelessness.

It's your experience

▶ 'My sister works in an Accident and Emergency department, and she says Friday and Saturday nights are a nightmare. You get the kids who've passed out because they've drunk so much, and others who are really badly hurt because they've been in an alcohol-related fight.'

Mel, aged 15

It's your opinion

▶ In many countries health services are provided free of charge. However some people think that people who damage their health through alcohol should be made to pay – after all it's their 'fault'. What do you think?

Many alcoholics become homeless, living rough in major cities all over the world.

▼

Violence and crime

Police studies suggest that alcohol is involved in half of all crimes. Alcohol-related crime includes offences against the licensing laws – such as selling or serving alcohol to under-age drinkers – being drunk and disorderly in public, and drink-driving. In the US, drink-driving is the leading drug-related crime. Alcohol is also often involved in violent crimes, such as assaults and criminal damage.

Drunken youths often get into fights outside pubs and clubs after heavy drinking.

Drunk and disorderly behaviour

Heavy drinking can make someone feel depressed, angry and out of control. Studies show that when young men have been drinking, they are more likely to see the behaviour of others towards them as challenging or insulting. One in four teenage boys get into fights after they have been drinking; one in ten get into trouble with the police.

It's your experience

'We came out of this club and there were three blokes standing there. They were obviously legless. One of them suddenly says to us, "What are you staring at?" It kicked off from there and the next thing, he'd smashed this bottle and there was blood running down my face. He'd glassed me. It was quite scary.'

Greg, aged 19

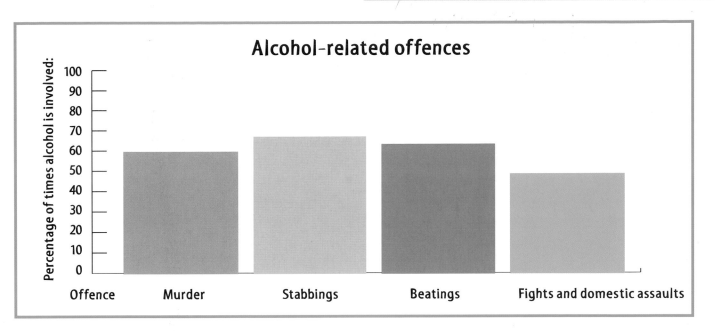

Alcohol-related offences

Percentage of times alcohol is involved:

Offence: Murder, Stabbings, Beatings, Fights and domestic assaults

Hot spots

Many incidents occur in city centres, shortly after pub or club closing times. Crowded drinking places, and cut-price drink promotions have been blamed for rising levels of crime, especially among young people.

In some countries alcohol also regularly causes disorder at football matches and other sporting events. It is often banned on coaches and trains carrying supporters to matches.

Drinking too much alcohol can cause problems with relationships and even violence in the home. ▶

Violent crime

Studies in the US show that alcohol is more closely related to violent crime than any other drug. In the UK, alcohol-related street violence has increased by almost 100 per cent in the past ten years. Every year, there are almost 1.5 million victims of violent attacks committed by people under the influence of alcohol.

Alcohol is also a major factor in cases of domestic violence. Almost half of all victims of violence in the home said their partner had been drinking.

It's your decision

Under-age drinking has been linked to rising cases of crime and disorder. Young people who drink heavily are more likely to commit alcohol-related offences than light drinkers, and they are also more likely to be the victims of crime.

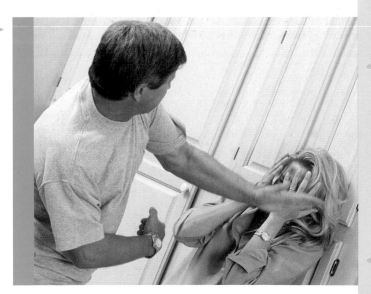

Alcohol and the law

Around the world, governments use a range of laws to control the making, selling and drinking of alcohol.

Men socialise without alcohol in a Muslim café in India. In some Indian states alcohol is forbidden.

Bans and controls

In seven countries all alcohol is forbidden by law on the grounds of religious (Muslim) faith. In a further 19 countries, alcohol can only be sold through state-run monopolies. Even in countries where alcohol is widely available, the law is used to control consumption by licensing sales outlets and enforcing minimum drinking ages and penalties for offences such as drink-driving. It is also used to ban or restrict alcohol advertising, and to raise taxes on alcohol sales.

Licensing laws

In many countries, special licences are needed for all premises selling alcohol. On-licences, such as pubs, clubs, and restaurants, are licensed to sell alcohol on the premises. Off-licences, such as shops and supermarkets, are licensed to sell alcohol for drinking elsewhere.

Licences enforce restrictions on the hours alcohol can be sold or consumed.

Some pubs and clubs try to protect their licences by employing door staff to ensure under-age drinkers are not allowed entrance.

Licences also set minimum drinking ages. These vary between countries, but are usually set between the ages of 17 and 21. A bar or restaurant owner could lose their licence if they illegally sell alcohol to under-age drinkers, and some countries have introduced proof of age cards to help enforce the law.

It's your experience

'When we have a night out, we don't take any chances. We share a taxi. It's not worth the risk of losing your licence.'

Kieran, aged 19

A police officer in Germany tests a driver's alcohol levels.

Police powers

In many countries, the police have powers to arrest and charge anyone who is 'drunk and disorderly' in a public place. They may also have powers to use breath and blood tests to enforce drink-driving laws. Some countries enforce a total ban on drink-driving. Others set legal limits for the amount of alcohol drivers can have in their bloodstream. Drivers who exceed the legal limit will be convicted, fined and have their driving licence taken away. If they have caused injury or death to anyone else, they may go to prison.

It's your decision

Alcohol slows down reflexes and reactions, and this makes drink-driving very dangerous. Legal limits vary in countries around the world, but some people argue that the only safe limit is no alcohol at all. Otherwise, people can underestimate the amount they have drunk.

Alcohol is big business

Alcohol today is big business: billions of pounds a year are spent on alcoholic drinks. The alcohol industry is a major employer in many developed countries, and provides governments with important revenues from taxes and exports.

Wine being bottled and packaged for export.

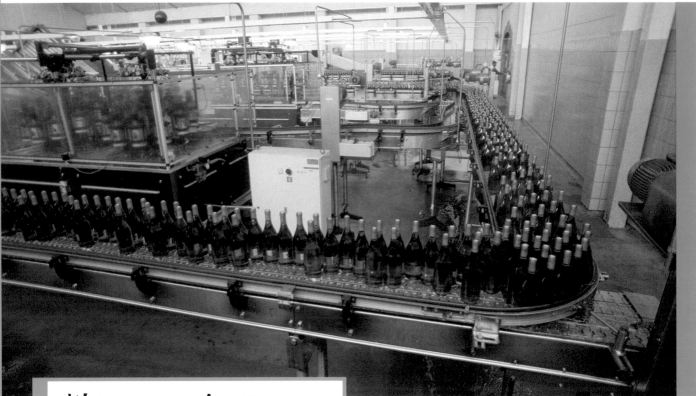

It's your experience

'Wherever you go in the world, you see the same brands – the same lagers, the same beers. You can be 2,000 miles from home, and drinking the same brand you'd drink at home. It's like fast food and burger bars – they're everywhere now.'

Matt, aged 16

Multinationals

In the last few decades, large multinational companies have increasingly taken control of the alcohol market, especially for beers and spirits. Between them, the top ten companies in the world sell around £200 billion of alcohol each year. They dominate the market because they can afford to spend heavily on advertising and marketing, and use new technologies to expand into new markets.

Many large manufacturers are now looking to expand their market and set up production in developing countries, like eastern Europe, where trade is opening up and creating new opportunities. The World Health Organisation recently published a report warning that alcohol-related problems now pose a greater threat to world health than tobacco, especially in developing countries, which may not have adequate public health education or regulations in place.

An advertisement for beer in China.

It's your opinion

Developing countries do not always have adequate controls on the advertising and marketing of alcohol. Some campaigns advertise alcohol as a tonic for young mothers or a product that promotes strength and health. Should there be tighter controls on marketing in the developing world?

Alcohol revenue

Taxing alcoholic drinks is a way of raising government revenue, and controlling consumption by cost. Taxes and duties on alcohol are an important source of revenue for many governments around the world. In Russia alcohol sales raise almost as much revenue for the government as the oil industry – about 24 billion roubles (£600 million) each year.

This can lead to a conflict of interest, as governments use alcohol to produce revenue, while still being concerned about the cost of alcohol to health and society.

The low taxes on alcohol in France encourage British day-trippers to go on 'booze cruises' to French hypermarkets.

Alcohol and the media

The alcohol industry spends billions of pounds each year advertising their brands. Adverts, merchandising, sports sponsorship, mobile phone messaging and the Internet are all used to reach target markets, especially young people.

The alcohol industry targets young people with sophisticated marketing strategies.

Lifestyle adverts

Alcohol advertisements and promotions often feature attractive young people drinking and having fun in glamorous places. The ads are often sexy, funny or witty, designed to appeal to target groups, such as women and teens. Positive images of people drinking are also sometimes shown in television programmes, selling the image that drinking is normal, fun and safe.

Targeting the young

Young people are an important target group for alcohol companies – they are the drinkers of the future. This means they have specific targeting strategies.

Websites promoting brands of alcohol use interactive games and competitions, free giveaways, screen-savers and chat rooms to encourage young drinkers. There are also 'point of sale' advertisements by cash tills in many convenience stores and petrol stations, where 75 per cent of teenagers shop weekly.

The alcohol industry uses the 4 'Ps' when marketing alcohol to young people:

• Products – alcopops and premium beers that appeal to young consumers

• Promotions – in teen magazines, and product placements in films rated PG and 12

• Places – alcohol outlets placed in college campuses and low-income areas

• Prices – some beers are now as cheap as soft drinks or bottled water

Advertising codes of practice

In many countries alcohol advertisers have to follow rules or 'codes of practice.' Some people believe that advertisers regularly ignore the codes and that there should be more restrictions on alcohol advertising, including websites and sports sponsorship.

The industry argues that advertising encourages people to try different brands, rather than to abuse alcohol. They point out that in France, where advertising alcohol is banned, the consumption of alcohol is higher than in other countries where advertising is allowed.

It's your experience

'You don't watch the ads and think, I'll buy that brand. You just see these really sexy girls and cool blokes and think I'd like some of that. And the drink lets you buy into it, a little bit.'

Kate, aged 18

It's your opinion

Some people think that advertising encourages people to drink more, but advertisers argue that it only encourages people to change brands. Which do you think is true?

Safe drinking messages

Many countries show adverts which warn against the dangers of drink-driving. Some people believe more money should be spent on 'safe drinking' messages as well. Recently, new campaigns warning against the dangers of binge drinking have been introduced, especially in holiday hotspots where alcohol often leads to public nuisance and violence.

A French billboard advertisement warning against the dangers of drink-driving.

jamais d'alcool au volant

DELEGATION A LA SECURITE ROUTIERE et LA PREVENTION ROUTIERE

Living with alcohol

Alcohol is a part of most people's lives, whether in small or large amounts. If we drink sensibly, alcohol can help us relax and enjoy ourselves with friends. But if we binge drink, or regularly drink too much, then alcohol can poison our bodies and harm our health. We may even become dependent on alcohol, as it is an addictive drug.

Alcohol doesn't solve problems – it just creates more.

Making our own decisions

Some people decide not to drink alcohol at all. This may be for health reasons, for personal reasons, such as a family history of alcohol abuse, or on religious grounds, if they are practising Muslims or Mormons for example.

It's your decision

Will alcohol make you forget?
When you are feeling stressed or unhappy, alcohol can seem an easy way of blotting it all out and avoiding your troubles. But the effect isn't lasting – and because alcohol is a depressant drug, it can make you feel a whole lot worse.

When alcohol becomes a problem

Drinking becomes a problem when we feel we are unable to relax or enjoy ourselves without alcohol. If we feel we are becoming too dependent on alcohol, we should try having a night out drinking non-alcoholic drinks to see if we can still have a good time – if we feel we can't, it may be a sign that we are already drinking too much alcohol.

It may then be time to take action, and perhaps seek some support from a counsellor, doctor or drink helpline.

Health rules

Even if we do want to drink alcohol regularly, we can take care of our health by following some simple rules. These include having some social life that is not focused on drinking, and not drinking alcohol alone or on impulse. We can decide to have some alcohol-free days in the week, and set ourselves a maximum weekly limit when we are drinking.

It's your experience

'I was on medication so I couldn't drink alcohol for a bit. At first it was really hard being out with my mates. They teased me a lot about it, but it made me realise I could have a good time without getting wrecked.'

Jamie, aged 19

When going for a night out, we can:

- eat before going out

- limit the amount of money we take

- take a drink buddy – that's one that makes sure we don't drink too much

- alternate alcoholic drinks with water or soft drinks (but not fizzy drinks)

A good night out

Many people socialise regularly without alcohol and still enjoy themselves. Having a good time should depend on how we are feeling, what we are doing, and who we are with - not what we are drinking.

▼ Our social lives don't need to revolve around alcohol.

Glossary

Addictive drug a drug that the body and mind can become dependent on

Binge drinking drinking heavily in one session: officially over 8 units in a session for a man, and over 6 units for a woman

Blood alcohol levels a measurement of alcohol carried in the bloodstream – also called blood alcohol concentration (BAC)

Cirrhosis liver disease which causes the loss of working liver cells as the liver shrinks and becomes more dense

Congeners substances added to give flavour, colour or smell

Dehydrate to dry out – alcohol causes dehydration because the kidneys take water from other body tissues to help flush out toxins from the body

Depressant drug a drug that depresses or slows down the central nervous system

Diuretic a substance that makes us pass more urine

Domestic violence violence that occurs in the home

ecstasy a chemically produced drug, usually in tablet form, which people take to produce happy feelings

Ethanol a compound of carbon, hydrogen and oxygen – the chemical name for alcohol

Fermentation a process in which yeasts work with sugars in fruit or grain to make alcohol and carbon dioxide

Gene a part of the make up of our bodies through which we inherit physical and other characteristics from our parents

Jaundice yellowing of the skin and other tissues in the body

Mead an alcoholic drink made from honey and water

Microbes minute life forms

Nutrients substances in food that our body needs to stay healthy

Osteoporosis brittle bones

Prohibition a total ban – a term used for a period when all alcohol was banned in the United States

Toxins poisons

Unsafe sex sex without using a condom, carrying the risk of pregnancy, and also HIV and other sexually-transmitted diseases

Further information

UK
Institute of Alcohol Studies
Offers information and a wide range of fact sheets on the use of alcohol.

Alliance House, 12 Caxton Street,
London SW12 OQS
Tel. 0207 222 4001
www.ias.org.uk

Alcohol Concern
National agency for alcohol misuse.

Waterbridge House, 32-36 Loman Street,
London SE1 OEE
Tel. 0207 928 7377
www.alcoholconcern.org.uk

The Portman Group
Leading UK alcohol producers who aim to encourage balanced understanding of alcohol-related issues.

7-10 Chandos Street,
Cavendish Square,
London WlG 9DQ
Tel. 0207 907 3700
www.portman-group.org.uk

Information on alcohol and drinking aimed at teenagers
www.wrecked.co.uk

USA
National Council for Alcohol and Drug Dependence
Lots of facts and information on alcohol and drug abuse.

20 Exchange Place,
Suite 2902,
New York NY 10005
Tel. 212/269 – 7797
www.ncadd.org

Australia
Australian drug information network (ADIN)
Provides links to Internet sites in Australia and the world that have useful information on alcohol and other drugs.

PO Box 818, North Melbourne
Victoria 3051
Tel. (3) 9278 8100
www.adin.com.au

The Australian Drug Foundation
Website of the Australian Drug Foundation, including a link to the Centre for Youth Drug Studies, which works to prevent drug and alcohol misuse.

(Postal address as for ADIN)
www.adf.org.au

Note to parents and teachers: Every effort has been made by the Publishers to ensure that these websites are suitable for children, that they are of the highest educational value, and that they contain no inappropriate or offensive material. However, because of the nature of the Internet, it is impossible to guarantee that the contents of these sites will not be altered. We strongly advise that Internet access is supervised by a responsible adult.

Index